Family Memories

When Your Grandad Was Little

Jane Bidder

Illustrated by Shelagh McNicholas

W
FRANKLIN WATTS
LONDON•SYDNEY

For my father, Michael Thomas, my father-in-law, John Bidder, and all grandads everywhere — J.B.

To Hannah, Tom and Sean — S.M.

The author and publisher wish to thank everyone who contributed their memories to this book.

First published in 2004 by Franklin Watts
96 Leonard Street, London EC2A 4XD

Franklin Watts Australia
45-51 Huntley Street, Alexandria, NSW 2015

Text © Jane Bidder 2004
Illustrations © Franklin Watts 2004

Editor: Caryn Jenner
Designer: James Marks
Art director: Jonathan Hair
Picture research: Diana Morris
Photography: Ray Moller unless otherwise credited.

Picture credits: Hulton Deutsch/Corbis: 13. Jim Marks: front cover clb, 25.
Picturepoint/Topham: front cover cla, 7,10,16,18, 22, 28cl, 28tr.

Every attempt has been made to clear copyright. Should there be any
inadvertent omission please apply to the publisher for rectification.

A CIP catalogue record for this book is available from the British Library.

ISBN 0-7496-5446-5

Printed in China

Contents

Changing times   6

Shopping   8

Tooth powder   10

Saturday cinema   12

Village picnic   14

Tweed coat   16

Steam train   18

Punch and Judy   20

Sailing to Britain   22

Box camera   24

First day at school   26

Timeline   28

Memories   29

Glossary and Index   30

Changing times

These pictures show children in
the present and in the past.

You are growing up
in the present.

Present ▼
This picture
shows a town in
the present.

Your grandad grew up in the past. Many things have changed since your grandad was a child.

In this book, lots of different grandfathers remember what it was like when they were little.

Shopping

"When I was little, I used to go to the shop with my mum. We gave our list to the shopkeeper, then he used a set of scales to weigh out the right amount of everything we needed."

The shopkeeper put weights on one side of the scales, and food on the other. When both sides were even, that was the right amount.

Soda crystals

Special offer

9

Tooth powder

"When I was little, I used to brush my teeth with tooth powder. First I put water on my toothbrush. Then I rubbed the wet toothbrush in the powder to make a paste."

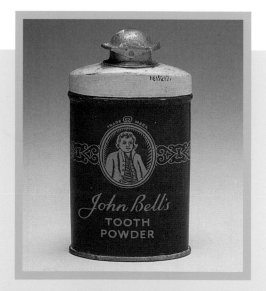

Some tooth powders came in a tin like this. You had to remember to put the lid on or the powder went hard.

Saturday cinema

"When I was little, I used to go to the cinema almost every Saturday to watch cartoons and cowboy pictures. On my birthday, all the other children in the cinema sang to me!"

Happy birthday to you...

Many children belonged to a cinema club, which cost about $2\frac{1}{2}$ pence a week. In between films, they often sang to music played on the organ.

Village picnic

"When I was little, we lived in India. Everyone in our village used to gather for a big picnic in the woods. We all brought lots of food to share, and after the picnic, we sang and danced."

Picnic foods included vegetable curry and sweet, sticky dumplings called gulab jamun.

14

15

Tweed coat

"When I was little, I wore a tweed coat, just like my father. I felt very grown up. But underneath my coat, I had to wear short trousers to school, even when it was cold!"

Tweed is a kind of wool. A tweed coat and cap were often part of a school uniform.

Steam train

"When I was little, I liked to go on a steam train. It was noisy and dirty and lots of fun! I watched the fireman stoke the coal in the engine, and the train driver let me pull the whistle."

The fire in the engine turned water into steam, which made the train move.

Punch and Judy

"When I was little, I liked watching Punch and Judy shows at the seaside.

Mr Punch was such a naughty puppet, but he made me laugh. Part of the fun was calling out to the puppets."

Over there! He's over there!

Punch and Judy are glove puppets. This Punch puppet has a face made of papier mâché.

21

Sailing to Britain

"When I was little, my family sailed from the Caribbean all the way across the ocean to Britain. The ship was huge! When we reached Britain, I was so excited! This was going to be my new home."

In the late 1940s and 1950s, thousands of people from the Caribbean Islands came to live in Britain.

Box camera

"When I was little, I had a box camera that took black and white pictures. I had to save up my pocket money to have the film developed, so I wanted every picture to be perfect. I loved taking photos!"

24

To take a picture with a box camera, you had to look through the glass lens, then click the metal lever.

First day at school

"When I was little, I was a bit scared on my first day at school. Then one of the bigger boys took me round, and I had a brilliant day! Now that I'm a grandad, I tell my grandchildren not to be scared. Some things haven't changed since I was young."

27

Timeline

This timeline shows the years from 1945 to 2010.

1945

1950

1960

The grandads in this book were children during the 1940s and 1950s.

1970

1980

During the 1960s and 1970s, these grandads became dads. This is when your mum and dad were probably children.

1990

2000

2010

You are a child now. What year were you born? When do you think you will be grown up?

Memories

Ask your grandad about when he was a child. Ask your teachers and other grown-ups about their memories, too. Here are some questions to ask.

What were your favourite toys and games?

How was your school different from mine?

What kinds of clothes did you wear?

What special events do you remember?

What things do we have now that you didn't have when you were a child?

Glossary

Memories   Things you remember from the past.
Do you have *memories* of your last birthday?

Remember   To think of the past.
Do you *remember* what you did yesterday?

Past   Time gone by. The *past* can mean yesterday
or it can mean a long time ago. Your grandad was
a child in the *past*.

Present   Now. Today is in the *present*. You are a child
in the *present*.

Timeline   A chart that shows the passing of time.
See the *timeline* on page 28.

Index

camera 24
cap 16
Caribbean 22
cinema 12, 13
coal 18
coat 16

engine 18

gulab jamun 14

India 14

photos 24
picnic 14
Punch and Judy 20
puppets 20

scales 8, 9
school 16, 26

seaside 20

ship 22
shopping 8
short trousers 16
steam train 18

timeline 28
tooth powder 10
tweed 16